How to Improve Your Listening Skills

Effective Strategies for Enhancing Your Active Listening Skills

I0462862

By Meir Liraz

Published by BizMove
www.bizmove.com

ISBN: 9781090104687

Table of Contents

MEIR LIRAZ

1. Introduction

Most of us are acquainted with the old riddle that goes: "If a tree falls in the forest, and no one is in the area to hear it, does it make a noise?" From a communication point of view, the answer must be a definite "No." Even though there are sound waves, there is no sound because no one perceives it. For communication to take place, there must be both a sender and a receiver. This guide is focused on the receiver - the one who provides feedback to the sender.

Saul Gellerman says: "The sender, to be certain that his message will be accepted by the receiver, must be prepared to let the receiver influence him. He must even be prepared to let the receiver alter or modify the message in ways that make it more acceptable to the receiver. Otherwise, it may not be understood or it may not be accepted, or it may simply be given lip service and ignored."

This places the responsibility for good communications squarely on the shoulders of both the sender and the receiver. Each of us plays the roles of sender and receiver many times each day. Thus, it is important to learn to play each role well.

Researchers have found that the average individual spends considerably more time each day in listening than in speaking, writing, or reading. Therefore, listening is a very important communicative skill.

Did you know that we devote about 40 to 45 percent of our working hours to listening? And did you know that, if you have not taken steps to improve this skill, you listen at only 25 percent efficiency? Putting these thoughts together, do you feel comfortable knowing that you earn 40 percent or more of your pay while listening at 25 percent efficiency? If not, perhaps acting on the information imparted in this chapter will improve your listening skills to above the average in listening efficiency. Tests have shown that we can significantly raise the level of our listening performance by a small amount of study and practice.

The importance of the listening skill to managers has been recognized by industrial firms for some time. Dr. Earl Planty, in his role as executive counselor at Johnson and Johnson, has said: "By far the most effective   method by which executives can tap ideas of subordinates is sympathetic listening in the many day-to-day informal contacts within and outside the work place. There is no system that will do the job in an easier manner. Nothing can equal an executive's willingness to listen."

Recognizing the value of effective listening, many companies offer training programs to improve this communicative skill. Some years ago the Methods Engineering Council compared one group of participants in a preliminary discussion on efficiency in listening with a second group not participating in such a discussion. The comparison was made by testing each group. The test results showed the marks made by the first group were 15 percent higher - a significant improvement.

2. What Listening Is

We hear - often without listening - when sound waves strike our eardrums. When we don't remember what we have heard, it is probably because we did not listen. A good example is the situation that frequently occurs when we are introduced to a new employee or a new acquaintance. A few minutes later we can't recall the person's name. Why? Because we probably failed to listen to the name when we were introduced.

Johnson defines listening as "the ability to understand and respond effectively to oral communication." Thus, we can state at the outset that hearing is not listening. Listening requires more than hearing; it requires understanding the communication received. Davis states it this way: "Hearing is with the ears, but listening is with the mind'."

Some of the attributes of a good listener are as follows:

He usually makes better decisions because the inputs he receives are better;

He learns more in a given period of time, thereby

saving time; and

He encourages others to listen to what he says because he appears more attentive and better mannered.

The typical listener, after 2 weeks can remember only 25 percent of what he has heard in a briefing or a speech. Therefore, listening is not effective for receipt and retention of factual details. For retention of factual details we must place our dependence on the written word.

Researchers have discovered that we can improve our listening comprehension about 25 percent. Most of us process the sender's words so fast that there is idle time for us to think about the message while it is being given. During this idle time a good listener ponders the sender's objectives, weighs the evidence being presented, and searches for ways to better understand the message. It follows that good listening can be considered "a conscious, positive act requiring willpower."

The ability to listen more effectively may be acquired through discipline and practice. As a listener you should physically and mentally prepare yourself for the communication. You must be physically relaxed and mentally alert to receive and understand the message. Effective listening requires sustained concentration (regardless of the length of the message), attention to the main ideas presented, note-taking (if the conditions are appropriate), and no emotional blocks to the message by the listener. You cannot listen passively and expect to retain the message. If you want to be an effective listener, you must give the communicator of the message sufficient attention and make an effort to understand his viewpoint.

3. Guides to Effective Listening

Here are some practical suggestions for effective listening which, if followed, can appreciably increase the effectiveness of this communicative skill.

Realize that listening is hard work. It is characterized by faster heart action, quicker blood circulation, and a small rise in body temperature. Researchers have found that the higher we climb on the organizational ladder, the more difficult listening becomes. In day-to-day conversations, show the communicator you are interested by looking and acting like you are.

Prepare to listen. To receive the message clearly, the receiver must have the correct mental attitude. In your daily communications, establish a permissive environment for each communicator.

Recognize your own biases. Learn what your biases are and channel them properly. You can then keep them from interfering with the message.

Resist distractions. Good listeners adjust quickly to any kind of abnormal situation; poor listeners tolerate bad conditions and, in some instances, may create distractions themselves. Take a clue from good listeners.

Keep an open mind. A good listener doesn't feel threatened or insulted, or need to resist messages that contradict his beliefs, attitudes, ideas, or personal values. Try to identify and rationalize the words or phrases most upsetting to your emotions.

Find an area of interest. Good listeners are interested and attentive. They find ways to make the message relevant to themselves and/or their jobs. Make your listening efficient by asking yourself: "What is he saying that I can use? Does he have any worthwhile ideas? Is he conveying any workable approaches or solutions? " G. K. Chesterton once said, "There is no such thing as an uninteresting subject; there are only uninteresting people."

Show some empathy. If we show some empathy, we create a climate that encourages others to communicate honestly and openly. Therefore, try to see the communicator's point of view.

Hold your fire. Be patient. Don't interrupt. Don't become over-stimulated, too excited, or excited too soon, by what the speaker says. Be sure you understand what the speaker means; that is, withhold your evaluation until your comprehension is complete. Mentally arguing with a communicator is one of the principal reasons so little listening takes place in some discussions. Don't argue. If you win, you lose.

Listen critically and delay judgment. Good listeners delay making a judgment about the communicator's personality, the principal points of the message, and the response. Ask questions and listen critically to the answers. Then, at the appropriate time, judgment can be passed in an enlightened manner.

Judge content, not delivery. We listen with our own experience. We do not understand everything we hear. It is not fair to hold the communicator responsible if we can't decode his message. One way to raise the level of our understanding is to recognize and assume our own responsibility.

Exercise your mind. Good listeners develop an appetite for hearing a variety of presentations - presentations difficult enough to challenge their mental capacities. Try it.

Capitalize on thought-speed. Most of us think at about four times faster than the communicator speaks. It is almost impossible to slow down our thinking speed. What do you do with the excess thinking time while someone is speaking? The good listener uses thought-speed to advantage by applying spare thinking time to what is being said. Your greatest handicap may be not capitalizing on thought-speed. Through listening training, it can be converted into your greatest asset.

F. S. Perls, author of Gestalt Theory Verbation, said, ". . . Don't listen to the words, just listen to what the voice tells you, what the movements tell you, what the posture tells you, what the image tells you."

4. Barriers to Effective Listening

There are several barriers to effective listening. According to Tortoriello, some of these barriers are as follows:

Recognizing that a personal risk is involved. Our thoughts and ideas might be changed in some way. Any change is threatening.initially;

Listening for only those things that are relevant to our own goals and objectives;

Listening for only those things that serve to satisfy our own needs;

Casting aside those things that don't conform to our own models of the world; and

Filtering the thoughts and ideas of the sender according to our frame of reference attitudes, beliefs, expectations, and relationship to the sender of the message.

Have you raised these barriers? Is the message coming directly to you without passing through some fine filters you have placed in the communications loop?

5. Limit Your Own Talking

This guide covering approaches to good listening would not be complete unless something was said about limiting our own talking while playing the role of receiver.

You cannot be an effective listener if you are too busy talking. Frank Tyget put it this way, "You can only improve on saying nothing by saying nothing often."

Following receipt of each oral communication, there is time for a response. As the receiver of the message, don't monopolize the conversation. Give the communicator an opportunity to respond to your comments. As the source of the message he should be given a chance to have the last word. If you give him that opportunity, he will feel important and believe he has communicated effectively. You, as the receiver, may feel justly that you have played your role as receiver well. Then, the communication can be considered truly effective.

6. Effective Listening Tips

Most people spend roughly 70% of their waking hours in some form of verbal communication. Yet, how many of us have ever had any formal training in the art of listening? Here are ten things you can do to improve your listening skills.

1. Approach the listening experience from a state of

To be centered is to be completely calm at a very deep level, to be without agendas or predispositions as to the outcome, and to be open to experience. Centeredness is a prerequisite to truly open listening. It sets the stage for the points below. For more on this topic, see Top Ten List #30, "Ten Ways to Develop Positive 'Ki' (Energy)"

2. Never rule out any topic of discussion as uninteresting.

Creative people are always on the lookout for new information. While some conversations may be completely inane, it's wise to make sure the subject is not worthwhile before tuning out completely.

3. Accept the speaker's message

On the face of it, this would seem to be an argument for gullibility--for believing almost anything anyone tells you. It's not. The point here is to withhold judgment during the immediate experience of listening. In accepting "as is", you're not making a determination as to the truth or falsity of the statement, you're simply acknowledging exactly what the speaker is saying--right or wrong, good or bad, true or false. This capacity for total acceptance frees the mind to listen for other clues, for example ...

4. **Listen for the whole message.**

One estimate has it that 75% of all communication is non-verbal. If you take away the words, what's left? Plenty, it turns out. Beyond the words themselves is a host of clues as to what the speaker is communicating. Some examples: posture (rigid or relaxed, closed or open); facial expression (does it support the words?); hands (clenched, open, relaxed, tense?); eyes (does the speaker maintain eye contact?); voice tone (does it match the words?); movement (are the speaker's movements intense, relaxed, congruent (with the message) or conflicting; do they suggest that the whole speech is "staged"?) What you're looking for here are inconsistencies between with is said and what is really meant, clues that tell you the spoken message isn't really genuine. Get the idea?

5. **Don't get hung up on the speaker's delivery.**

Then there are factors that simply reveal an awkwardness in delivery rather than any attempt to mislead. The key is being able to distinguish between the two. It's easy to get turned off when someone speaks haltingly, has an irritating voice, or just doesn't come across well. The key to good listening, however, is to get beyond the manner of delivery to the underlying message. In order for this to happen, you have to resolve not to judge the message by the delivery style. It's amazing how much more clearly you can "hear" once you've made the decision to really listen rather than to criticize.

6. **Avoid structured listening.**

It's popular among some communications teachers to recommend a format for listening, either in the form of questions ("What is the speaker's main point? What is he/she really saying?) or key words (e.g., purpose, evidence, intent). The problem with this approach is that it creates a dialogue of noise in the listener's mind which interferes with clear reception. Better to operate from the openness of the centered state (above) and receive the information just as it comes, without any attempt to structure or judge it. Think of your mind as similar to the central processing unit of a computer in which the data comes in and is stored without change, available for subsequent access.

7. **Tune out distractions.**

Poor listeners are distracted by interruptions; good listeners tune them out and focus on the speaker and the message. It's a discipline that lends itself to specific techniques for maintaining one's focus. Here are some things that will help: Maintain eye contact with the speaker; lean forward in your chair; let the speaker's words "ring" in your ears; and turn in your chair, if necessary, to block out unwanted distractions.

8. **Be alert to your own prejudices.**

This goes along with #3 above, but it's so important that you may want to think specifically about the impact of your prejudices on your ability to really hear what's being communicated. Often, we are unaware how strongly our prejudices influence our willingness and ability to hear. The fact is: any prejudice, valid of not, tends to obscure the message.

9. **Resist the temptation to rebut.**

Why is it that, when we hear someone saying something with which we strongly disagree, we immediately begin mentally formulating a rebuttal? Many reasons, but one of the most common is our natural tendency to resist any new information that conflicts with what we believe. Keep in mind: you can always rebut later, when you've heard the whole message and had time to think about it.

10. **Take notes sparingly.**

The world seems to be split between those who take prolific notes and those who take few or none, with each side equally strong in its position. I come down toward the latter view for this reason: the more focused you are on writing down what is being said, the more likely you are to miss the nuances of the conversation. There are two good ways around this dilemma. You can write down only key words and then, after the conversation, meeting, etc., go back and fill in, or you can take notes pictorially, that is, by diagramming what the speaker is saying. It's a technique called, "mind-mapping" and it was first popularized by a writer named Tony Buzan well over a decade ago in a book entitled, "Use Your Head". You may want to look up his books; he's written several.

Closing Comments

Are you an effective (good) listener? Do you listen intently and try to understand what the sender means? Do you try to put your understanding of the message in your own words and feed back what you feel the communicator meant - without adding to or deleting anything from the message?

If so, you will reach a better understanding with the originator of the message. Are you willing to enter the communicator's world for a few moments and share his experiences through intensive listening? By so doing, you can become an effective listener and convey a great kindness to him. At that point, you have taken a positive step toward improving your ability to communicate with others.

HOW TO IMPROVE YOUR LISTENING SKILLS

MEIR LIRAZ

www.ingramcontent.com/pod-product-compliance
Lightning Source LLC
Chambersburg PA
CBHW072312170526
45158CB00003BA/1288